CREATIVE CHRISTMAS CAROLS

How to personalize your own piano arrangements

Arranged by Gail Smith

CONTENTS

ISBN 978-1-4768-0850-5

HAL•LEONARD®
CORPORATION
7777 W. BLUEMOUND RD. P.O. BOX 13819 MILWAUKEE, WI 53213

In Australia Contact:
Hal Leonard Australia Pty. Ltd.
4 Lentara Court
Cheltenham, Victoria, 3192 Australia
Email: ausadmin@halleonard.com.au

Visit Hal Leonard Online at
www.halleonard.com

PERFORMANCE NOTES

SILENT NIGHT IN CHIMES (p. 4)

Create the Sound of Bells–Learning to Chime

Silent Night is written in chimes with the right hand playing the melody and an interval of a 4th down and the left hand playing the melody and a 6th down. Keeping your hands in a fixed hand position enables you to chime with ease. When you play the chimed melody two octaves higher and hold the damper pedal down, the effect is very beautiful. Follow the same formula and play *Joy to the World* and *The First Noel* (p. 5) in the same way and create the sound of bells chiming carols. Any melody may be played as a chime using this easy formula.

AWAY IN A MANGER (p. 6)

Creative Left-hand Patterns

Using the best left-hand accompaniment for the melody is important. Six left-hand patterns are shown for carols in 3/4 time. *Away in a Manger* is written out using many of these patterns. This carol is written out using the key of G and then in the key of F.

IT CAME UPON THE MIDNIGHT CLEAR (p. 8)

Decorate with Musical Ornaments

Using trills, turns, mordents and grace notes, the carols can be embellished using these musical techniques. Placing one musical ornament on the first or third beat of the melody sounds best. Play through this carol as written, then change the placement of the grace notes and trills or turns, creating your own arrangement. Place the ornaments carefully and leave space between them just like ornament balls on your tree.

GOOD CHRISTIAN MEN, REJOICE (p. 10)

Decorate with Pentatonic Patterns

There are six black-key patterns that can be used with this carol, *Good Christian Men, Rejoice*. There could be as many as 120 different patterns using five notes. The melody is in the bass clef and could be doubled by playing as an octave. A violin or flute could play along on the melody while several pianists play different patterns on the pentatonic cluster of black keys. The possibilities are endless for having fun with this song! I have had ten pianists playing it at the same time, everyone using their own pattern on the black keys and several playing the melody.

SILENT NIGHT (p. 12)

Decorate with a Special Fill

This arrangement uses an easy right-hand fill. To create this fill on any chord, you simply start on the fifth note of the chord and use the first three consecutive notes of the name of the chord. So as the example shows on p. 12: for a C chord you start on G and then play the notes C-D-E. This fill sounds fabulous going up and down and using it as an introduction before the melody comes in. It will glisten around the melody like a stream of expensive garland around your tree.

ANGELS WE HAVE HEARD ON HIGH (p. 14)

Decorate with Scales

It is interesting to think of the intervals that make up a song and watch for those spots that have a half note followed by one step up. When I find this happens in a song this is what I do: I play a one-octave scale using 16th notes and then land on the melody note. It makes a very smooth fill that fits into many songs. This same concept can be used if there is a note that gets two counts followed by a step down. Simply play a scale down to the next melody note. Decorating with a scale in between melody notes is fun and is like a shining string of sparkling lights going up the branches of your Christmas tree. Try using the scale fill in measure 20.

HARK! THE HERALD ANGELS SING (p. 16)

Embellish with Octave-jump Scales

When there are three consecutive quarter notes in a melody, you may jump an octave higher and descend with a scale. In the third measure of this carol, you may use this special fill and play the same fill as written out. There are so many times you will be able to use this embellishment, so practice this pattern and be aware of the melody so that you can add this decoration to your song.

PAT-A-PAN (p. 18)

Decorate with a New Beat

Change the left-hand beat in a heartbeat with any of the eight patterns on the top of the page. You can also use them as an introduction to this beloved Christmas song. Perhaps you might play an extended ending too if you like. Customize this piece with your choice of left-hand patterns.

WE WISH YOU A MERRY CHRISTMAS (p. 20)

Creative Endings

We Wish You a Merry Christmas is arranged going from 3/4 time to 4/4 time. Several optional endings are given for you to choose from. It is often hard to decide what to put on the top of your tree. Do you want a fancy cluster of ribbons, an angel on top or a glittering star? Enjoy choosing which ending you want to use for this song, or any of the other carols you play.

O COME, ALL YE FAITHFUL (p. 22)

In this arrangement of *O Come, All Ye Faithful*, many fills and patterns are used. The introduction uses perfect fourths for a dramatic effect. There are many spots where the two-beat scale can fill in at measures 10, 15, 16, 22, 24, 30, 35, 36, 44 and 45 to name just a few. In measure 34, there is a four-beat fill with a two-octave scale going down a half step first. This four-beat fill fits because there are four beats to the next measure and that note is the SAME as the note in the previous measure taking you from D to D. In measure 32, there are consecutive upward steps that connect the melody. In measure 51 you could use the fill for steps walking down.

Merry Christmas and a Happy New Year to you!
–GAIL SMITH

Create the Sound of Bells

Learning to Chime

Chime a scale; next play it two octaves higher

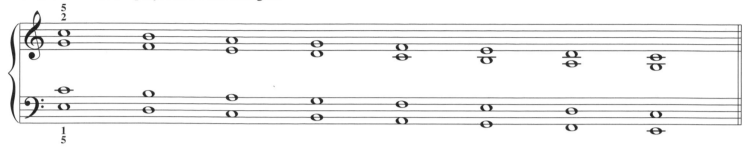

Tips:
1. The R.H. plays the melody with a note a 4th below, while the L.H. plays the melody with a note a 6th below.
2. Play two octaves higher.
3. Use the same fingering throughout.
4. Hold the pedal down throughout.

Silent Night in Chimes

Music by Franz X. Gruber

Joy to the World

Music by George Frideric Handel

Decorate each melody note with a chime.

The First Noel

17th Century English Carol
Music from W. Sandys' *Christmas Carols*

Decorate each melody note with a chime.

Creative Left-hand Patterns

Six left-hand patterns for 3/4 time

Away in a Manger

Music by James R. Murray

(Use left-hand patterns ①, ② and ③)

Away in a Manger

Music by James R. Murray

(Use left-hand patterns ④, ⑤ and ⑥)

Decorate with Musical Ornaments

It Came Upon the Midnight Clear

Music by Richard Storrs Willis

Decorate with Pentatonic Patterns

R.H. accompaniment pattern (5 3 4 2 3 1) starting on 3 different notes.

Good Christian Men, Rejoice

14th Century German Melody

Decorate with a Special Fill

Form the fill on any chord.

On a C chord, start on the 5th of the chord, then the 1st, 2nd, and 3rd notes.

Silent Night

Music by Franz X. Gruber

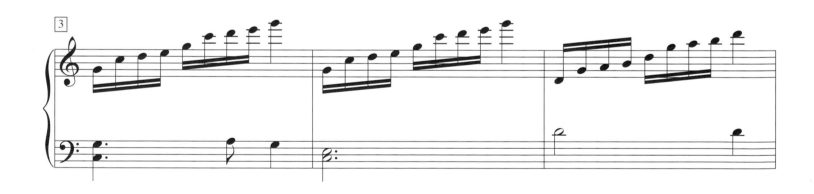

Decorate with Scales

When the melody is a half note followed by a step up or down, play a scale in between.

Angels We Have Heard on High

Traditional French Carol

mf

With pedal

Embellish with Octave-jump Scales

When there are two beats followed by the same note, you may fill in with an octave jump followed by a scale.

Hark! The Herald Angels Sing

Music by Felix Mendelssohn-Bartholdy

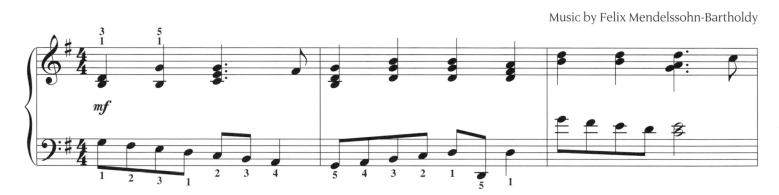

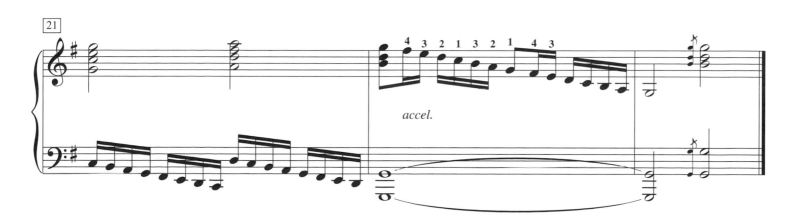

Decorate with a New Beat

Choose any of these accompaniment patterns to create a drum effect.

Pat-a-Pan
(Willie, Take Your Little Drum)

Words and Music by
Bernard de la Monnoye

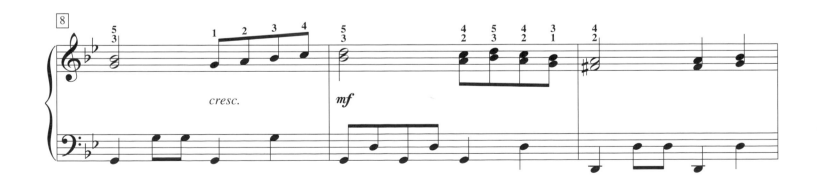

Creative Endings

Choose one ending you wish from the following options:

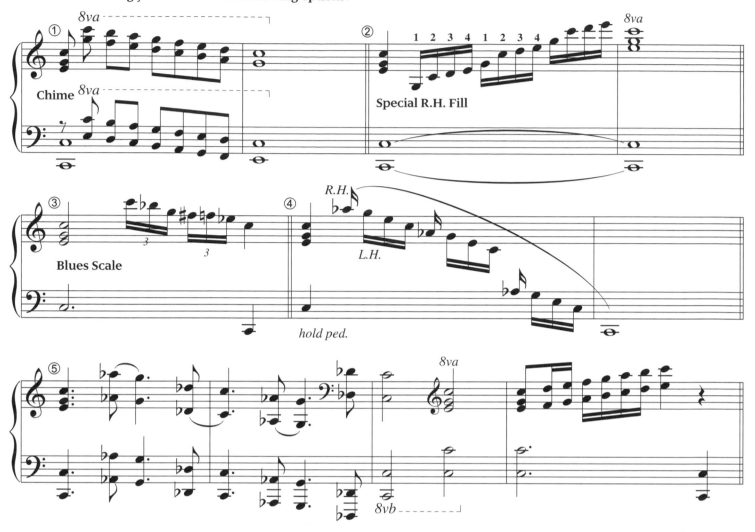

We Wish You a Merry Christmas

Traditional English Folksong

O Come, All Ye Faithful

(Adeste Fideles)

Music by John Francis Wade